For Mike with thanks for all
of your help and support;
and Courtney who shows me the
possibilities for childhood.

This book is the private
property of its owner. The
information that is drawn
or written in this book
is for that person and
a trusted adult.

All families keep secrets. Some families keep good secrets. Good secrets you only keep for a short time like keeping a suprise party a secret from your brother or sister... or baking a cake for your Dad's birthday. These secrets feel good to keep inside.

Some families keep bad secrets. Someone in your family like
Mom or Dad, an older brother or sister or housekeeper
or babysitter may tell you to keep this secret.

2

You might be told to keep this secret so that person won't get into trouble. That person might also tell you that it would hurt other family members if found out, or that you have done something bad and could get into trouble, too.

This kind of secret feels scary to tell, because that person in your family is supposed to take care of you and protect you.

4

Instead, this person
in your family may
touch you or kiss you
or play games with
your body. This person
may tell you to do
these things to
their body.

Doing these things might make you feel yucky. You might feel mixed-up, sad, or angry, maybe ashamed or scared. Maybe you might feel all of these things.

6

These feelings are much different
from hugs and closeness by adults
who do love you and respect your
needs and rights as a person.

7

You can't keep
carrying this secret.
It's too big for one
person.
500 lbs.

8

You need to find an
adult who is not a member
of your family to help you
solve this problem.

This could be a teacher you like and trust, a school counselor, a coach, or a minister, if you go to church.

These people can listen,
and respect, and believe
the secret you need to tell.
They can get other adults
to help protect you and
help solve your problem,
so you can stop carrying
this secret that feels
so awful.

11

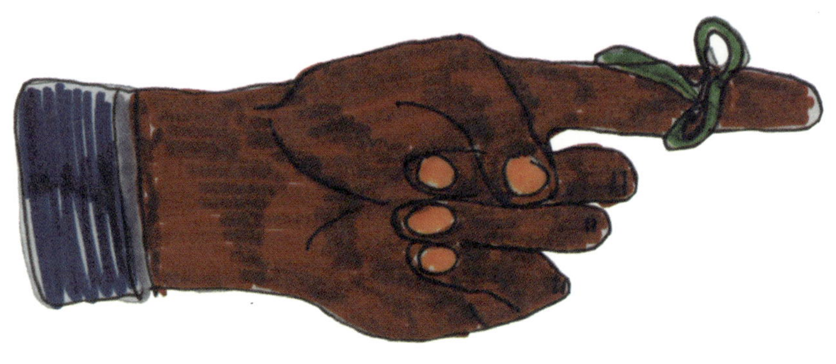

Here are two things you need to remember
to keep telling yourself:

    1. It Is Not My Fault.

    2. I Will Still Be Loved.

Here are some things that you
can do to help tell your secret so that
a trusted adult can help you . . .

13

In the picture below, make yourself one of
the characters. Draw on the faces and name
the other character or characters. Draw in body
parts to help explain what happened. Tell
what the person was wearing. Draw more in the
picture as you need to to tell what happened.

14

You can write out what happened. Try to remember
what the person may have said to you. Where were you?
What did this person tell you to do? Where were other
family members? What feelings do you have about
what happened to you?

17

You can draw a picture or pictures about what happened to you. Explain more details if you can as you talk about your drawings with your trusted adult.

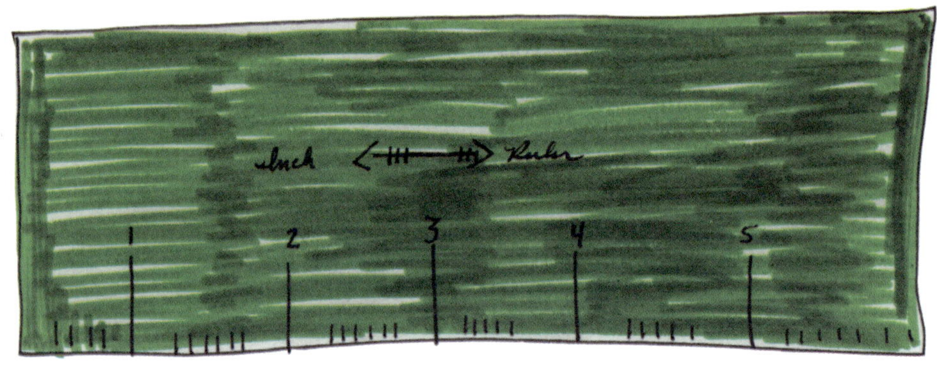

You might have to tell what happened
a little bit at a time.

You might have bad dreams at night.
It might be hard to concentrate on
school or play during the day.

These are all ways your body tries
to help you remember the things that you
need to talk over, write, or draw out
with your trusted adult.

22

So, at your own pace, tell your trusted adult what happened to you and remember...

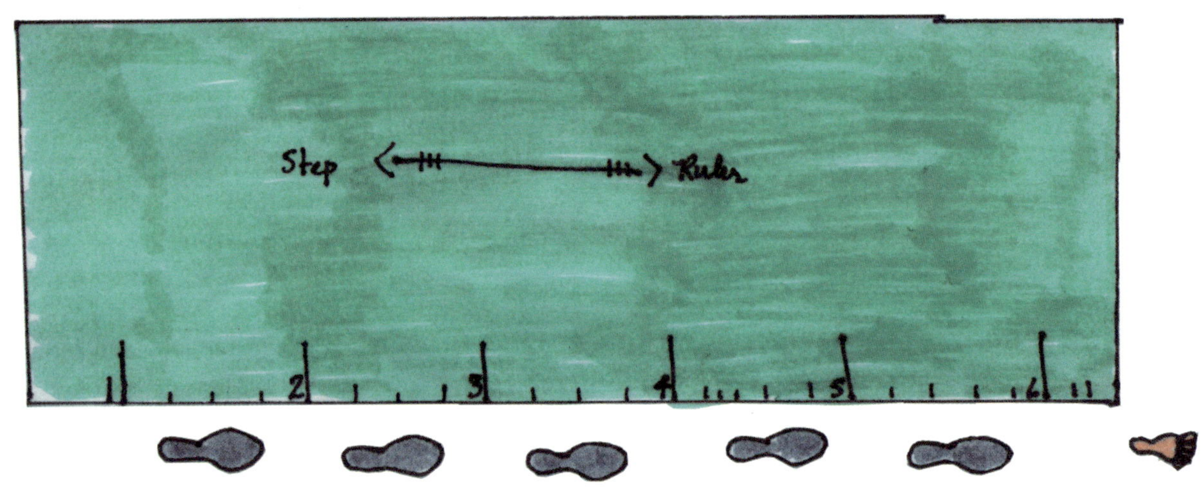

As you tell a little bit, one step at a time, you will begin to let go of the secret and begin to feel better.

You know you are feeling better when you
want to eat at a favorite place with friends,
or when you begin smiling and laughing again,
or when you stop thinking so much about
your secret.

I'll feel better when:

____

____

2. _______________________________

____

3. _______________________________

____

4. _______________________________

____

You can make your own list here. Write down all of those things that will let you know you are feeling better.

26

Another
List :
1.
2.
3.
4.
5.

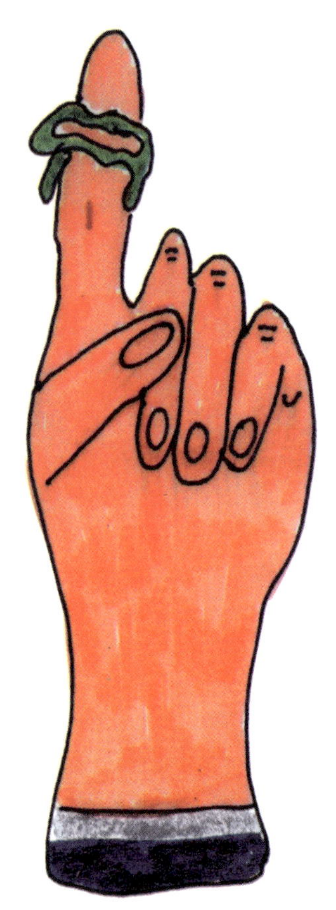

No matter how much of your secret
you feel safe telling your trusted
adult, you must always remember:

    1. IT IS NOT YOUR FAULT.

    2. YOU ARE STILL LOVED.

30